2 Volume — The Metropolis of Tokyo

Here are the symbols used in this textbook.

□ ····· New Problem

? ····· Aims of Learning

★ ····· Hints for Thinking

! ····· Summary of Learning

○ ····· Practice Problems

2 Volume   Tokyo

5 Congruent   Nima Town,
Shapes   Shimane Prefecture

5 Congruent
Shapes

5 Congruent
Shapes

Whole Numbers and Decimal Numbers

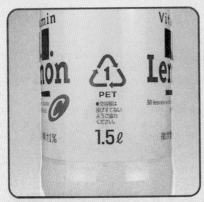

Regular Gas

Liters

The width between goal posts in soccer
7.32m

The weight of one grain of rice
0.02g

4

The length of Onaruto Bridge
1.629km

Decimal numbers are used for many things.

The distance in a marathon
42.195km

Let's learn the structure for expressing whole numbers and decimal numbers!

1 Structure of the Numeration System

1 ❷ Let's find out the structure of the number 42.195!

4 2 . 1 9 5

Place Place Place Place Place

☐ ☐ ☐ ☐ ☐

1 What does the 4 in the tens place mean? How many of what does this digit represent? Also, let's find out about other numbers!

5

💡 42.195 has the following structure:

$$42.195 = \quad 10 \quad\ \times 4 \ \cdots\cdots\ 40$$
$$+\ \ 1 \quad\ \times 2 \ \cdots\cdots\ 2$$
$$+\ \ 0.1 \quad \times 1 \ \cdots\cdots\ 0.1$$
$$+\ \ 0.01 \ \times 9 \ \cdots\cdots\ 0.09$$
$$+\ \ 0.001 \times 5 \ \cdots\cdots\ \underline{0.005}$$
$$42.195$$

2 Fill in the ⬚ for the following equation.
$$605.9 = 100 \times \boxed{} + 10 \times \boxed{} + 1 \times \boxed{} + 0.1 \times \boxed{}$$

By using the numbers from 0 to 9 and a decimal point, you can express all kinds of whole numbers and decimal numbers.

Let's make many different numbers on the calculator!

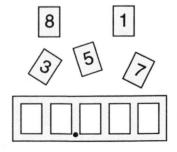

① Please place the cards on the right in the boxes to make the greatest number. Also, make the smallest number.

8   1

3   5   7

□ □ . □ □ □

► **Numbers that are** 10 **times,** 100 **times,** $\dfrac{1}{10}$ **and** $\dfrac{1}{100}$
as large, and the place of their decimal points

2 🔢 Please find how the position of the decimal point changes when you multiply 2.385 by 10 and 100.

$$2.385 \times 10 \;=\; \boxed{}$$

$$2.385 \times 100 = \boxed{}$$

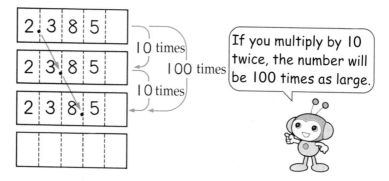

> If you multiply by 10 twice, the number will be 100 times as large.

1   What number is 1000 times as large as 2.385? How does the decimal point move?

💡 When you multiply a whole number or decimal number by 10, 100, ... , the decimal point moves 1, 2, ... places to the right.

1   Find the numbers that are 10 and 100 times as large as the following numbers.
   (1) 4.072   (2) 0.54   (3) 83

2   What number do you multiply 2.78 by to get the following numbers?
   (1) 278   (2) 27.8   (3) 2780

3 ❓ Find out how the decimal point moves if you make a number that is $\frac{1}{10}$ and $\frac{1}{100}$ of 238.5.

$$238.5 \div 10 = \boxed{}$$

$$238.5 \div 100 = \boxed{}$$

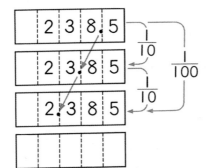

By dividing twice by 10, the number is divided by 100.

① Find the number that is $\frac{1}{1000}$ of 238.5. How will the decimal point move?

❗ If you make a number that is $\frac{1}{10}$, $\frac{1}{100}$, ... of a whole number or decimal number, the decimal point will move 1, 2, ... places to the left.

① Find $\frac{1}{10}$ and $\frac{1}{100}$ of the following numbers.

(1) 341.9   (2) 9.8   (3) 710

② What fraction do you multiply 39.7 by to make the following numbers?

(1) 0.397   (2) 3.97   (3) 0.0397

Let's Figure Out the Following Interesting Calculations Using a Calculator!

$1 \times 9 + 2 =$ ☐

$12 \times 9 + 3 =$ ☐

$123 \times 9 + 4 =$ ☐

$1234 \times 9 + 5 =$ ☐

$12345 \times 9 + 6 =$ ☐

$123456 \times 9 + 7 =$ ☐

$1234567 \times 9 + 8 =$ ☐

Start with ☐1 and press 3 numbers on your keypad counter-clockwise to make a 3-digit number. Then add the next 3-digits to the first one. Repeat by going around the keypad.

$123 + 369 + 987 + 741 =$ ☐

Try starting from ☐2 and going clockwise.

9

2 Estimating Products and Quotients

1 ❓ 183 fifth and sixth grade students went to a nature park by bus. Each student paid 735 yen for the bus. What is the total cost of the bus?

① Estimate the product by rounding 735 and 183 to the highest place of each number.

To round a number to the highest place, you look at the digit in the second highest place, don't you?

② Please compare the estimated product with the actual value of 735×183 by using a calculator.

2 ❓ In the nature park, there is a rectangular field with an area of 1034m^2. One of its sides is 47m long. How many is the estimated length of the other side of the field?

① Estimate the quotient by rounding 1034 and 47 to the highest place of each number.

② Use a calculator to find the actual value of 1034÷47, and compare it with the estimated quotient.

To estimate a product or a quotient, you usually round the numbers to their highest places.

1 Find the approximate values of the following calculations, then use the calculator to find the actual values.

(1) 8130×698   (2) 2870×9210   (3) 83.7×196

(4) 97310÷185   (5) 581064÷3124   (6) 870.4÷512

 **Check**

1 Fill in the ⬭ for the following equations.

(1) 8723 = 1000 × ☐ + 100 × ☐ + 10 × ☐ + 1 × ☐

(2) 4.605 = 1 × ☐ + 0.1 × ☐ + 0.01 × ☐ + 0.001 × ☐

2 What numbers are 10 times and 100 times as large as 0.162?

3 What are the numbers $\frac{1}{10}$ and $\frac{1}{100}$ of 5.23?

At the end of the unit,
write down the following in your notebook.

◎ What you understood and felt good about

◎ What things are similar to what you learned before

◎ What you would like to learn in the future

It will be useful if you write down what you thought about after each unit.

2 Volume

How much larger is box C than box A?

If you compare them by the number of cartons of milk, box C is ⬭ packs larger than box A.

Sayuri

We could measure the area by using 1cm² squares. I wonder if we can do something similar for the size of a box.

1cm

1cm

Makoto

Let's learn how to measure the size of rectangular prisms and cubes!

1 Volume

1 ❷ Which of the following boxes is larger and by how much? Think about how to show the size of each box.

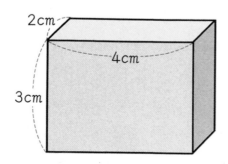

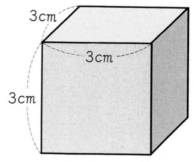

se cubes with 1 cm edges to build the same shaped rectangular prism and cube that appeared on the previous page.

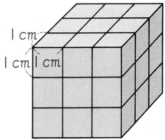

2 How many cubes did you use for each box?

! The size of rectangular prisms and cubes can be expressed as the number of cubes with 1 cm edges.

The amount of space an object takes up is called **volume**.
The volume of a cube with a 1 cm edge is 1 **cubic centimeter** and is written as 1 cm³.

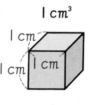

3 What are the volumes of the rectangular prism and the cube on the previous page? Which shape is larger and by how much?

1 What are the volumes of the following shapes?

(1)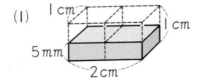

(2)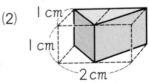

2 Volume of Rectangular Prisms and Cubes

1 **?** Let's think about how to calculate the volume of the rectangular prism on the right!

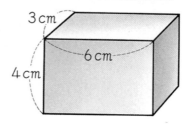

3 cm
6 cm
4 cm

We could find the area using length x width . . .

Mami

1 Find how many 1cm^3 cubes are in the rectangular prism.

❶ How many cubes fit into the length of the first layer?

❷ How many cubes fit into the width of the first layer?

❸ How many layers are there?

2 Find how many cubes there are in the rectangular prism by calculation.

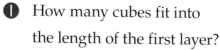

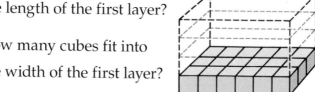

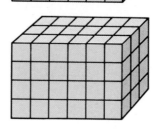

The number of 1cm^3 cubes in the rectangular prism above is:

$$3 \times 6 \times 4 = 72$$

Because there are seventy-two 1cm^3 cubes, its volume is 72cm^3.

3 Find the volumes of the rectangular prism and the cube on page 13 by calculation.

To calculate the volume of a rectangular prism or a cube, follow the steps below:

❶ Measure the length, width, and height of the rectangular prism or cube.

❷ Multiply the three values above.

You can find the volumes of rectangular prisms and cubes with the following formulas.

Volume of a rectangular prism = Length × Width × Height
Volume of a cube = 1 edge × 1 edge × 1 edge

1 How many cm^3 are the volumes of the rectangular prism and the cube below?

(1)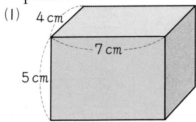
4 cm
7 cm
5 cm

(2)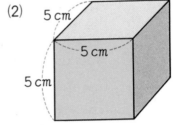
5 cm
5 cm
5 cm

2 Find ways to calculate the volume of the rectangular prism on the right.

When the units for each edge are different . . .

Naoko

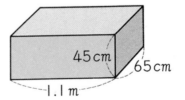
45 cm
65 cm
1.1 m

16

▶ **Ideas for finding volume**

2 🔢 Let's think about how to find the volume of the shape on the right!

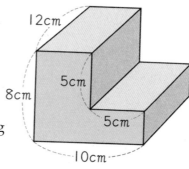

① Please explain the following two people's solutions.

Ritsuko

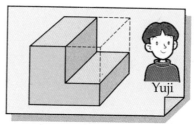

Yuji

② Find the volume using the two methods above.

3 Let's investigate how the volume changes when the height changes from 1 cm to 2, 3, or 4 cm without changing the width and length of the figure on the right!

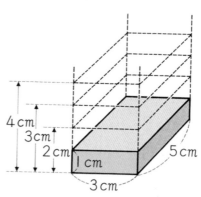

① Complete the table below and investigate the results.

Height(cm)	1	2	3	4
Volume(cm³)				

② When the height becomes 2 times, 3 times, and 4 times as much as 1 cm, how does the volume change?

17

Practice 1

① A rectangular prism was made by putting together six layers of 1cm cubes as shown on the right. What is the volume of the rectangular prism in cm^3?

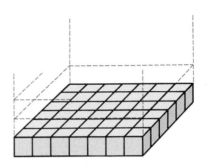

② Please find the volumes of the cube and the rectangular prism below.

(1)

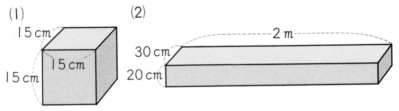

15 cm
15 cm
15 cm

(2)

2 m
30 cm
20 cm

③ Please find the volume of the figure on the right.

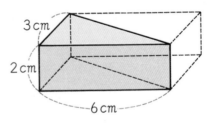

3 cm
2 cm
6 cm

④ Please find the volumes of the figures below.

(1)

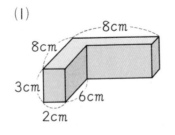

8cm
8cm
3cm
6cm
2cm

(2)

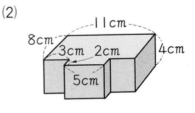

8cm
11 cm
3cm 2cm
5cm
4cm

3 Units for Large Volumes

1 ❓ Let's think about how to show the volume of the rectangular prism on the right!

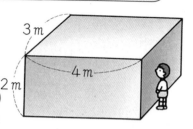

3 m
4 m
2 m

Kazuya

> For large areas, we use an area unit made out of a square with 1 meter sides . . .

💡 To show a large volume, you use a unit made out of a cube with 1m edges.

1 m³
1 m
1 m
1 m

The volume of a cube with 1m edges is called 1 **cubic meter** and is written as 1m³.

① What is the volume of the rectangular prism above?

① What is the volume of a cube which has an edge of 2m in cm³?

2 What is 1m³ in cm³?

① How many 1cm³ cubes are there in a 1m³ cube?

$$100 \times 100 \times 100 = 1000000$$

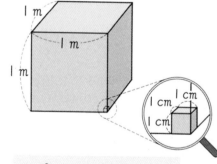

1 m
1 m
1 m
1 cm
1 cm
1 cm

1 m³ = 1000000 cm³

① How many m³ is the volume of a rectangular prism with a length of 3m, a width of 3m, and a height of 200cm? How many cm³ is it?

4 Capacity

1 We made a container with a 1cm thick board that looks like the rectangular prism on the right. Let's find the volume of water that fits in the container!

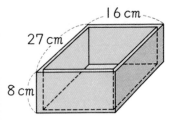

16 cm
27 cm
8 cm

1 To find the volume of water that fits in the container, what dimensions do you need to know?

The dimensions of the inside of a container are called the **inside measure**. The height of the inside of a container is called the depth. The size of the inside of a container is called **capacity** and it shows the volume of water needed to fill it.

Capacity

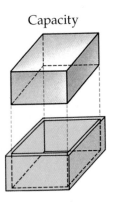

2 What are the inside measures (length, width, and depth) of the container above? How many cm^3 is the capacity?

1 What is the capacity of a water tank with an inside measure of 2m length, 3m width, and 1m depth?

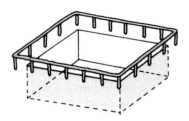

2 The capacity of a container that has an inside measure of **10cm** each for length, width, and depth is **1ℓ**. Let's look at the figure below and find the relationship between the units for volume and capacity!

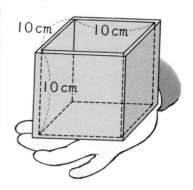

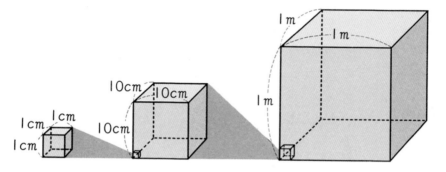

⭐ **1** How many cm^3 is 1ℓ? Also, how many $mℓ$ is 1ℓ?

$$1ℓ = 1000\,cm^3$$

$$1ℓ = 1000\,mℓ$$

$1cm^3 = 1mℓ$

Mami

2 How many ℓ is $1m^3$?

I wonder how many cm^3 is $1m^3$.

$$1m^3 = 1000ℓ$$

Minoru

❶ How many cm^3 is $1dℓ$?

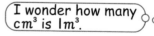

It was . . .
$$1dℓ = \frac{1}{10}ℓ$$

▶ Approximate capacity

3 A lunch box looks like the one on the right. Let's find the approximate capacity of this lunch box!

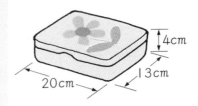

1 What does the shape of this lunch box look like?

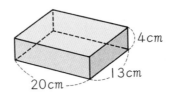

$13 \times 20 \times 4 =$ ☐

Answer :about ☐ cm^3

① A bathtub looks like the one on the right. What is the approximate capacity of this bathtub in ℓ?

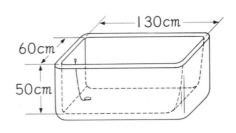

② Let's estimate the capacity of your classroom!
  Also, find the approximate capacity of many different things around you.

Practice 2

① What are the volumes of the following rectangular prism and cube?

(1)

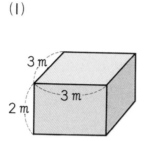

(2)

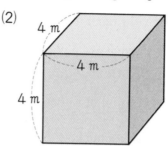

② The inside measures of the length and width of the water tank on the right are as indicated. We filled it with water up to a depth of 20cm. How many ℓ of water were put in it?

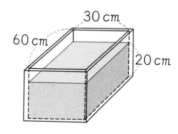

Challenge

Can You Measure the Volume of a Round-shaped Rock?

How can I measure the volume of a round-shaped object such as a rock?

The water level goes up by the same amount as the volume of the rock.

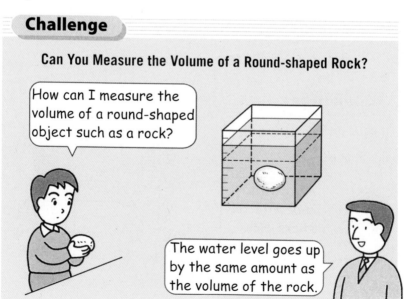

23

1. Please fill in the boxes with the appropriate units.

   (1) The volume of a cube with 1cm edges is 1⬭.

   (2) The capacity of a cube with inside measures of 10cm length, 10cm width, and 10cm depth is 1⬭.

   (3) The volume of a cube with 1m edges is 1⬭.

2. Please think about how to find the volume of the rectangular prism on the right. Then fill in the boxes.

   3cm · 5cm · 4cm

   (1) 3 cubes with 1cm edges fit in the length, and 5 cubes with 1cm edges in the width. So the first layer will have ⬭ cubes. The height is 4cm so you need to make ⬭ layers.

   (2) The total number of 1cm³ cubes can be found by the caluculation of ⬭×⬭×⬭ . So the volume of this rectangular prism is ⬭ cm³.

Challenge

How Many People Can Fit in the Space?

Make a 1m³ cube with 1m sticks. How many children can fit in it?

24

R e v i e w · 1

① Please calculate.

(1) $0.49 + 0.839$ (2) $7.53 + 2.47$ (3) $4.345 + 1.7$

(4) $0.93 - 0.631$ (5) $1.3 - 0.39$ (6) $7 - 2.87$

(7) $\dfrac{7}{9} + \dfrac{5}{9}$ (8) $\dfrac{8}{11} + 2\dfrac{6}{11}$ (9) $2\dfrac{3}{5} - \dfrac{1}{5}$ (10) $1\dfrac{1}{3} - \dfrac{2}{3}$

② Please find the estimated value of the following calculations. Then use a calculator to find the actual value.

(1) 748×521 (2) 840×326 (3) 461×304

(4) $5742 \div 319$ (5) $6678 \div 106$ (6) $3395 \div 485$

③ Using the digits 1, 3, 5, and 9 only once, and a decimal point, make the largest possible number and the smallest possible number.

④ The figure on the right is the net of a cube. When you fold it back into a cube, which faces will be parallel to each other? Which faces will be perpendicular to edge AB?

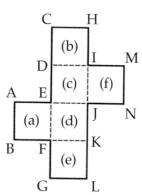

⑤ Please calculate. For division calculations, divide completely.

(1) 0.2×3 (2) 3.6×2 (3) 13.6×6 (4) 2.3×54

(5) $3.2 \div 4$ (6) $6.5 \div 5$ (7) $15.4 \div 7$ (8) $51.6 \div 43$

3 Multiplication of Decimal Numbers

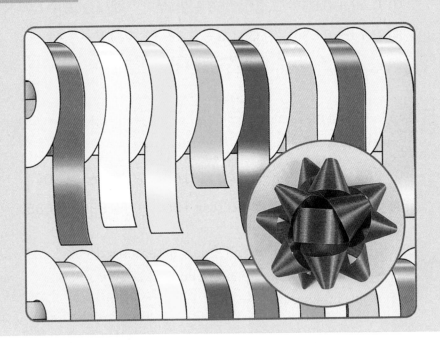

1 Multiplying by a Decimal Number

1 We bought 3.4 meters of ribbon that cost 180 yen per meter. What was the price of the ribbon?

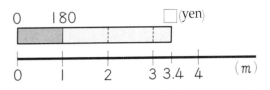

What is the math sentence for the price of 3m of the ribbon?

❓ How should we write the math sentence?

$$\boxed{\text{Price for } 1m} \times \boxed{\text{Length we bought (Unit: } m)} = \boxed{\substack{\text{Price we} \\ \text{have to pay}}}$$

Let's think about multiplication of decimal numbers!

💡 Even if the length of the ribbon is shown as a decimal number, we can construct a multiplication sentence just like we do with whole numbers to find the price of the ribbon.

$$180 \times 3.4$$

❓ Let's think about how to calculate 180×3.4!

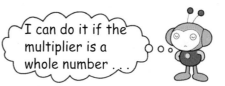

I can do it if the multiplier is a whole number . . .

1 Let's explain these two friends' methods!

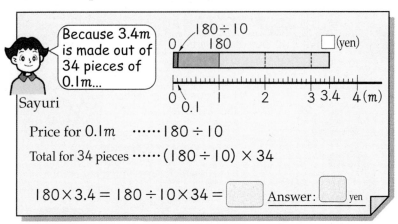

Sayuri

Because 3.4m is made out of 34 pieces of 0.1m...

Price for 0.1m ······ 180 ÷ 10

Total for 34 pieces ······ (180 ÷ 10) × 34

$180 × 3.4 = 180 ÷ 10 × 34 = \boxed{}$ Answer: $\boxed{}$ yen

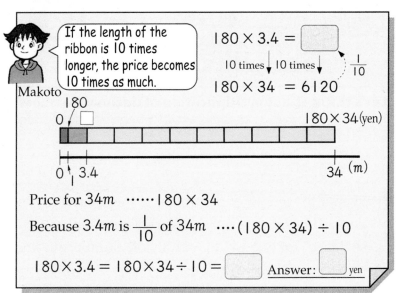

Makoto

If the length of the ribbon is 10 times longer, the price becomes 10 times as much.

$180 × 3.4 = \boxed{}$

10 times ↓ 10 times ↓ $\frac{1}{10}$

$180 × 34 = 6120$

Price for 34m ······ 180 × 34

Because 3.4m is $\frac{1}{10}$ of 34m ···· (180 × 34) ÷ 10

$180 × 3.4 = 180 × 34 ÷ 10 = \boxed{}$ Answer: $\boxed{}$ yen

Both of them came up with the idea of using whole numbers to do the calculation.

1 If we buy 2.7m of ribbon that costs 240 yen per meter, what will the price be?

▶ Algorithm for decimal multiplication

2 There is a 1m pipe that weighs 2.17kg. How much would 2.8m of the pipe weigh?

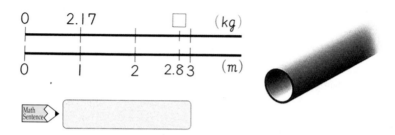

Math Sentence	

1 Let's think about how to do the calculation!

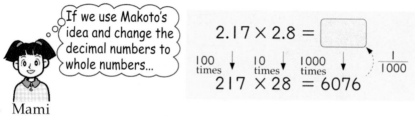

If we use Makoto's idea and change the decimal numbers to whole numbers...

Mami

$2.17 \times 2.8 = \boxed{}$

100 times ↓ 10 times ↓ 1000 times ↓ $\frac{1}{1000}$

$217 \times 28 = 6076$

The product of 2.17×2.8 can be found by multiplying two numbers that are 100 times 2.17 and 10 times 2.8, and then dividing the product by 1000.

$$2.17 \times 2.8 = 6.076 \qquad \text{Answer: } 6.076\,kg$$

? Let's think about how to calculate 2.17×2.8 with the multiplication algorithm!

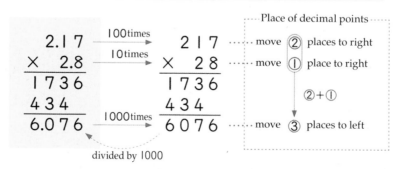

```
  2.1 7   100 times    2 1 7
×   2.8   ─────────→  ×   2 8
          10 times   
  1 7 3 6              1 7 3 6
  4 3 4                4 3 4
  6.0 7 6  1000 times  6 0 7 6
          ─────────→
```

divided by 1000

····· Place of decimal points ·····

···· move ② places to right

···· move ① place to right

②+①

···· move ③ places to left

ℹ️ How to carry out multiplication when the multiplier is a decimal number

❶ Carry out the calculation as if there were no decimal points.

❷ To determine the location of the decimal point of the product, add the number of places that are to the right of the decimal points of the multiplicand and the multiplier. Then move the decimal point of the product from right to left the same number of places.

```
    2.1 7 ------- ② places
  ×   2.8 ------- ① place
  1 7 3 6
  4 3 4           ②+①
  6.0 7 6 ------- ③ places
```

① (1)
```
    4.3 7
  ×   5.6
```
(2)
```
    3.8 1
  ×   7.4
```
(3)
```
    4 8.7
  ×   3.1
```

(4) 9.6×9.52 (5) 4.8×2.64 (6) 0.41×6.83

3 ❷   Let's think about how to carry out the following two calculations!

(1)
```
    4.9 2
  ×   7.5
    2 4 6 0
  3 4 4 4
  3 6.9 0 0
```

(2)
```
    0.0 1 8
  ×     3.4
      7 2
    5 4
  0.0 6 1 2
```

① (1) 2.35×5.6 (2) 5.48×3.65 (3) 0.37×2.7

(4) 0.36×1.25 (5) 54×6.8 (6) 875×5.12

▶ Multiplier and the size of the product

4 There is a ribbon that costs 180 yen for 1m. We want to buy two strips of that ribbon. One strip is 1.8m and the other one is 0.8m. Which strip of ribbon costs less than 180 yen?

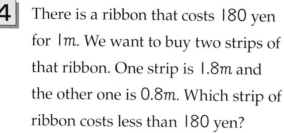

? Let's think about the relationship between the multiplier and the size of the product!

(1) 180 × 1.8 = ☐

(2) 180 × 0.8 = ☐

1 Which one of the products becomes smaller than 180?

! In multiplication of decimal numbers, if the multiplier is less than 1, the product will be less than the multiplicand.

If multiplier > 1, then the product > multiplicand
If multiplier < 1, then the product < multiplicand

1 Which of the following produces a product that is smaller than 6?
Ⓐ 6 × 0.9   Ⓑ 6 × 1.4   Ⓒ 6 × 2.08   Ⓓ 6 × 0.85

2 (1) 83 × 0.7   (2) 29.3 × 0.4   (3) 0.98 × 0.8

▶ Rules of formulas and calculations

5 🅱 Let's find out if we can use the formulas for area and volume, even if the lengths of the sides are shown with decimal numbers!

(1) The area of a rectangle that has a length of 2.3cm and a width of 3.6cm

‹--3.6cm--›

2.3cm

① How many squares with 1mm sides are in this rectangle?

② When we have 100 squares with 1mm sides, it becomes 1cm². How many cm² is the area of the rectangle?

③ Please find the area of the rectangle by calculating 2.3×3.6.

(2) The volume of a rectangular prism that has a length of 0.8m, a width of 1.2m, and a height of 0.7m

0.8 m

0.7 m

1.2 m

④ Calculate the volume by using centimeters and meters as units, then compare the results.

💡 Even if the lengths of the sides are shown with decimal numbers, we can find area and volume by carrying out the multiplication calculations indicated by formulas.

① What is the area of a postcard that has a length of 10.3cm and a width of 14.8cm?

6 Let's find out if the calculation rules we found for whole number calculations work for calculating decimal numbers!

(1) ■ × ● = ● × ■

(2) (■ × ●) × ▲ = ■ × (● × ▲)

(3) (■ + ●) × ▲ = ■ × ▲ + ● × ▲

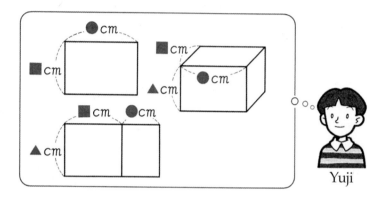

Yuji

⭐ 1 Please put decimal numbers in the ■ , ● , and ▲ , and find out if rules (1) , (2) , and (3) work.

Let's put 2.5 for the ■ , 3.4 for the ● , 4.2 for the ▲ .

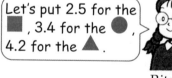

Ritsuko

The calculation rules we found for whole numbers apply to the calculation of decimal numbers.

① Please carry out the following calculations by thinking about better ways to calculate.

(1) 4.8 × 4 × 2.5

(2) 2.4 × 1.8 + 2.6 × 1.8

Practice

① Please calculate the following problems. Also, please check your work with a calculator.

(1) 7.2×36.5 (2) 1.63×4.9 (3) 0.15×29.7

(4) 21.6×16.2 (5) 6.97×18.4 (6) 5.66×1.28

(7) $1.3 \times 2.5 \times 8.4$ (8) $1.57 \times 3.8 \times 4.5$

(9) $3.6 \times 1.2 + 1.4 \times 1.2$ (10) $5.8 \times 0.45 - 1.36$

② The weight of 1ℓ of milk is $1.03kg$. If we pour 0.18ℓ of this milk into a cup, what is the weight of the milk in the cup in kg?

③ There is a water tank that looks like the figure on the right. What is the capacity of the tank in m^3?

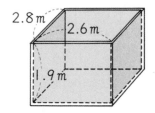

2.8 m   2.6 m   1.9 m

④ We bought two strips of ribbon. Each one is $2.3m$ in length. One of them cost 160 yen for $1m$ and the other one cost 240 yen for $1m$. Then we gave 1000 yen to the cashier. What is the change?

⑤ There is a $1m$ pipe that weighs $1.8kg$. Please write a word problem that has 1.8×0.8 as its math sentence.

2 Times as Many/Much and Multiplication

1 There are several tapes like the ones shown on the right. If we make the length of the red tape the base unit, how many times as long as the red tape are the other tapes?

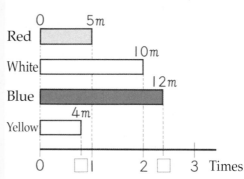

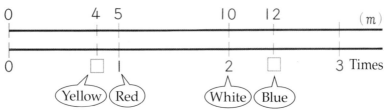

1 How many times as long is the blue tape as the red tape?

The white tape is 2 times as long as the red tape.

Math Sentence ▷ [ ]

Answer : [ ] times

2 How many times as long is the yellow tape as the red tape?

Math Sentence ▷ [ ]

Answer : [ ] times

The word "times" can be used with decimal numbers that are less than 1.

35

2 There is a 5m strip of red tape. There are also a brown tape and a green tape. The length of the brown tape is 3.5 times as long as the red tape. The length of the green tape is 0.6 times as long as the red tape.
Please find the length of the brown tape and the green tape.

? Think about what we need to do to find the size of something when it is expressed as a decimal number of times.

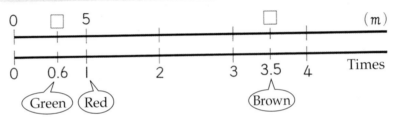

1 What is the length of the brown tape?

The length that is 3.5 times as long as 5m is the length that corresponds to 3.5 when we consider 5m as 1.

$$5 \times 3.5 = \boxed{}$$ Answer: $\boxed{}$ m

2 What is the length of the green tape?

Math Sentence ⟩ $\boxed{}$ Answer: $\boxed{}$ m

💡 To find something that is 3.5 times or 0.6 times of the given size, you multiply the given size by 3.5 or 0.6.

1 Please find the capacity of a tank that will hold 4.2 times and 0.8 times as much as a 7ℓ tank.

36

 **Check**

1. Please find the mistakes in the following calculations and make corrections.

(1)	(2)	(3)
8.1	0.07	5.74
× 3.4	× 0.14	× 2.5
324	28	2870
243	7	1148
275.4	0.098	1.4350

2. Please calculate the following problems.

(1) 1.3 × 4.8   (2) 0.42 × 6.5   (3) 0.82 × 0.72

3. Please find the weight of two bags that are 1.5 times and 0.75 times as heavy as a 5.6kg bag.

Challenge

Let's Try a Mysterious Multiplication Calculation!

❶ Select a decimal number

❷ Multiply the number by 0.25

❸ Multiply the result by 0.625

❹ Multiply the result by 12.8

❺ Multiply the result by 0.5

What is the result of the calculations?

3.2 × 0.25 = ☐

☐ × 0.625 = ☐

☐ × 12.8 = ☐

☐ × 0.5 = ☐

4 Division of Decimal Numbers

3 m 420円   2. 8m420円

3 m 420円   2. 8m420円

1 Dividing by a Decimal Number

1 When we bought 2.8m of ribbon, the price was 420 yen.
How much was the price of 1m of ribbon?

0   □   420(yen)

0   1   2   2.8 3   (m)

If the price of 3m of ribbon is 420 yen, the price for 1m would be . . .

? How should we write the math sentence?

| Price we paid | ÷ | Length we bought (Unit: m) | = | Price for 1m |

Let's think about how to divide a number by a decimal number!

Even if the length of the ribbon is shown with a decimal number, we can construct a division math sentence just like we do with a whole number to find the price of 1m of ribbon.

$$420 \div 2.8$$

Let's think about how to calculate $420 \div 2.8$!

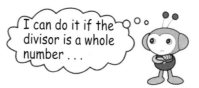

I can do it if the divisor is a whole number . . .

1 Let's explain these two friends' methods!

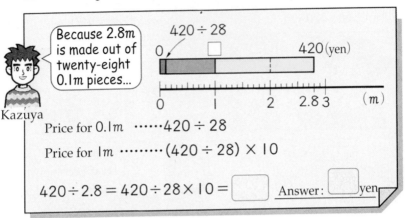

Kazuya

Because 2.8m is made out of twenty-eight 0.1m pieces...

$420 \div 28$

420 (yen)

Price for 0.1m ······ $420 \div 28$

Price for 1m ········· $(420 \div 28) \times 10$

$420 \div 2.8 = 420 \div 28 \times 10 = \boxed{}$ Answer: $\boxed{}$ yen

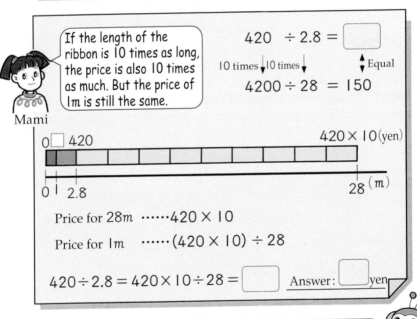

Mami

If the length of the ribbon is 10 times as long, the price is also 10 times as much. But the price of 1m is still the same.

$420 \div 2.8 = \boxed{}$

10 times / 10 times   Equal

$4200 \div 28 = 150$

420×10 (yen)

Price for 28m ······ 420×10

Price for 1m ······ $(420 \times 10) \div 28$

$420 \div 2.8 = 420 \times 10 \div 28 = \boxed{}$ Answer: $\boxed{}$ yen

Both of them came up with the idea of using whole numbers to do the calculation.

① The price for 3.5m of ribbon was 630 yen. What would be the price for 1m of ribbon?

▶ Algorithm for decimal division

2 There is a 6.2m pipe that weighs 7.44kg. How much would 1m of pipe weigh?

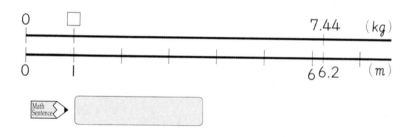

Math Sentence ▷ [ ]

1 Let's think about how to do the calculation!

If we use Mami's idea and change the decimal numbers to whole numbers...

Makoto

$$7.44 \div 6.2 = \boxed{}$$

10 times ▼ 10 times ▼ ↕ Equal

$$74.4 \div 62 = 1.2$$

The quotient of $7.44 \div 6.2$ is equal to the quotient of $74.4 \div 62$ because both the dividend and divisor were multiplied by 10.

$$7.44 \div 6.2 = 1.2$$

Answer: 1.2 kg

2 Let's think about the calculation of $7.44 \div 6.2$ using the algorithm!

6.2)7.44

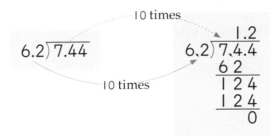

10 times

$6.2\overline{)7.44}$

10 times

$$6.2\overline{)7.4.4} \quad \begin{array}{r} 1.2 \\ \hline 7.4.4 \\ 6\,2 \\ \hline 1\,2\,4 \\ 1\,2\,4 \\ \hline 0 \end{array}$$

⚡ How to carry out the division algorithm when the divisor is a decimal number

❶ Move the decimal point of the divisor to the right and make it a whole number.

❷ Move the decimal point of the dividend to the right the same number that you moved the divisor.

❸ Carry out the calculation just as if the divisor were a whole number. Then place the decimal point of the quotient right above the decimal point of the dividend that was moved to the right.

$$6.2\overline{)7.4.4} \quad \begin{array}{r} 1.2 \\ \hline 7.4.4 \\ 6\,2 \\ \hline 1\,2\,4 \\ 1\,2\,4 \\ \hline 0 \end{array}$$

① (1) $4.2\overline{)7.56}$ (2) $2.8\overline{)8.96}$ (3) $3.7\overline{)9.731}$

(4) $3.84\overline{)9.216}$ (5) $2.37\overline{)9.954}$ (6) $7.3\overline{)58.4}$

3 ❷ Let's think about how to carry out the following three calculations!

(1) $2.368 \div 3.7$ (2) $8.4 \div 3.36$ (3) $7 \div 1.25$

$$3.7\overline{)2.3.6\,8} \quad \begin{array}{r} 0.6\,4 \\ \hline 2.3.6\,8 \\ 2\,2\,2 \\ \hline 1\,4\,8 \\ 1\,4\,8 \\ \hline 0 \end{array}$$

$$3.36\overline{)8.4\,0} \quad \begin{array}{r} 2.5 \\ \hline 8.4\,0 \\ 6\,7\,2 \\ \hline 1\,6\,8\,0 \\ 1\,6\,8\,0 \\ \hline 0 \end{array}$$

$$1.25\overline{)7.0\,0} \quad \begin{array}{r} 5.6 \\ \hline 7.0\,0 \\ 6\,2\,5 \\ \hline 7\,5\,0 \\ 7\,5\,0 \\ \hline 0 \end{array}$$

① (1) $5.04 \div 8.4$ (2) $2.738 \div 3.7$ (3) $5.9 \div 2.36$

(4) $92.3 \div 1.42$ (5) $6 \div 2.5$ (6) $42 \div 5.6$

▶ Divisor and the size of the quotient

4 The white ribbon costs 240 yen for $1.2m$ and the blue ribbon costs 240 yen for $0.8m$.

Which ribbon costs more for $1m$?

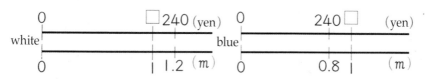

❷ Let's find the relationship between the divisor and the size of the quotient!

(1) $240 \div 1.2 = \boxed{}$

(2) $240 \div 0.8 = \boxed{}$

1 Which quotient becomes larger than 240?

❗ For division of decimal numbers, when you divide by a number smaller than 1, the quotient becomes larger than the dividend.

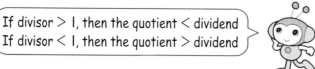

If divisor $>$ 1, then the quotient $<$ dividend
If divisor $<$ 1, then the quotient $>$ dividend

① Which of the following produces a quotient larger than 8?

Ⓐ $8 \div 1.25$ Ⓑ $8 \div 0.02$ Ⓒ $8 \div 0.64$ Ⓓ $8 \div 5$

② (1) $19.8 \div 0.3$ (2) $0.39 \div 0.6$ (3) $69 \div 0.92$

▶ Size of remainder

5 We are going to put 2.5ℓ of juice into a 7dℓ capacity bottle.

How many bottles can we fill? How many ℓ of juice will be left over?

2.5 ℓ

❷ Let's think about division calculations that involve a remainder!

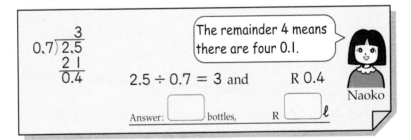

1

First, changing the unit to dℓ . . .

$25 \div 7 =$ ▢ R ▢

Answer: ▢ bottles, R ▢ ℓ

Minoru

$$0.7\overline{)2.5}$$
$$\underline{2\ 1}$$
$$0.4$$

The remainder 4 means there are four 0.1.

$2.5 \div 0.7 = 3$ and R 0.4

Answer: ▢ bottles, R ▢ ℓ

Naoko

2 Please check the answer by changing Naoko's math sentence into "divisor × quotient + remainder = dividend."

💡 The decimal point of the remainder should line up with the original decimal point of the dividend.

$$0.7\overline{)2.5}\quad \rightarrow\quad 0.7\overline{)2.5}$$
$$\underline{2\ 1}\qquad\qquad \underline{2\ 1}$$
$$4\qquad\qquad\ 0.4$$

1 Please calculate and find the quotient to the $\frac{1}{10}$ place. Also, please find the remainder.

(1) $17.58 \div 9.6$ (2) $46.37 \div 2.45$ (3) $34 \div 72.5$

▶ Quotient of rounded numbers

6 We are planning to build a flower garden that has an area of $7.2m^2$. If we make the width $2.9m$, then how many m should the length be? Please round off the number to the second highest place.

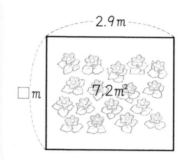

2.9 m

☐ m

$7.2m^2$

1 Please make the length ☐ m and construct a multiplication math sentence. Then find the answer.

$$\square \times 2.9 = 7.2$$
$$7.2 \div 2.9 = 2.48\overset{5}{\cdots}\cdots$$
       Answer: about $2.5\, m$

1 1.5ℓ of sand weighs $2.6kg$. How many kg does 1ℓ of sand weigh? Please round the answer to the second highest place.

Practice

① Please calculate. For division calculations, divide completely. Also, check the answer using a calculator.

(1) $62.9 \div 3.7$　　　(2) $5.76 \div 7.2$　　　(3) $3.24 \div 1.08$

(4) $1.62 \div 2.16$　　　(5) $0.779 \div 8.2$　　　(6) $12.21 \div 1.65$

(7) $4.2 \times 3.5 \div 2.8$　　　　(8) $13.6 \times 0.6 \div 1.6$

② 6.5ℓ of oil weighs $5.2kg$.

How much does 1ℓ of oil weigh in kg?

③ We bought $32m$ of rope to make jump ropes.
How many jump ropes can we make if the length of each jump rope is 2.5 m?
How many m will be left over?

④ A flower garden has a length of $3.6m$ and a width of $8.5m$.

If we keep the area of the flower garden the same and make the width $1.7m$ shorter, how many m should the length be?

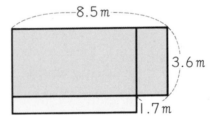

⑤ A pipe weighs $1.8kg$.

Please make up a word problem in which the math sentence would be $1.8 \div 1.2$.

2 Times as Many/Much and Division

1 We have measured the distance from our houses to the train station.

If we make Yoshiko's distance as the base unit, how many times as far are the other people's houses from the station?

Distance from a house to the train station

Name	Distance (km)
Yoshiko	2.4
Akira	4.8
Michiko	3.6
Kiyoshi	1.8

? Let's think about what kind of calculation we need to find how many times as far!

1 How many times as far from the station are Michiko and Kiyoshi's houses as Yoshiko's house?

Akira's house is 2 times as far as Yoshiko's house.

Michiko
Math Sentence⟩ [　　　　　]   Answer: [　] times

Kiyoshi
Math Sentence⟩ [　　　　　]   Answer: [　] times

1.5 times as far means that when we look at 2.4km as the base unit of 1, 3.6km is the same as 1.5.

💡 Even when decimal numbers are involved, we use division to find how many times as much a quantity is, compared to the size of the base unit.

2 Akira's father weighs 63kg. He is 1.8 times as heavy as Akira.
What is Akira's weight in kg?

❓ Let's think about the kind of calculation we need to find the size of the base unit!

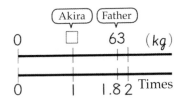

1 Let's construct a multiplication sentence by setting Akira's weight to ☐ kg! Then, please find the number that goes in the ☐.

Math Sentence ⟩ [ ]   Answer: [ ] kg

💡 When you find the size of the base unit, it is easier if you construct a multiplication sentence using a ☐.

1 There is a thermos that has a capacity of 1.5ℓ. It is 0.6 times the capacity of a kettle.
How many ℓ is the capacity of the kettle?

Check

1 Please find the mistakes in the following calculations and make corrections.

(1) 5.41 ÷ 1.3 　(2) 75.4 ÷ 1.16 　(3) 2.1 ÷ 2.8

```
          4.1
    1.3)5.4.1
        5 2
          2 1
          1 3
         0.8
```

```
            6.5
    1.16)7 5.4
         6 9 6
           5 8 0
           5 8 0
               0
```

```
           7.5
    2.8)2.1 0
        1 9 6
          1 4 0
          1 4 0
              0
```

2 Please divide completely.

(1) 5.74 ÷ 0.7 　　(2) 12 ÷ 7.5 　　(3) 3.6 ÷ 4.8

3 How many times as much as $6.4m^2$ are $43.2m^2$ and $1.6m^2$?

Challenge

Let's Try a Mysterious Division Calculation!

❶ Select a decimal number
❷ Divide the number by 1.6
❸ Divide the result by 0.5
❹ Divide the result by 1.25

What is the result of the calculations?

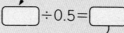

4.2 ÷ 1.6 = ▭

▭ ÷ 0.5 = ▭

▭ ÷ 1.25 = ▭

What kind of calculation is it going to be?

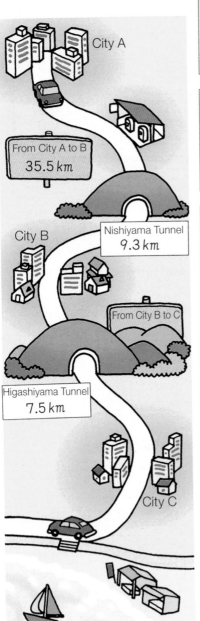

City A

From City A to B
35.5 km

City B

Nishiyama Tunnel
9.3 km

From City B to C

Higashiyama Tunnel
7.5 km

City C

We bought 37.5ℓ of gasoline that cost 108 yen for 1ℓ.
How much was the total price?

Nishiyama Tunnel is how many times as long as Higashiyama Tunnel?

The distance between City B and City C is 1.4 times as long as the distance between City A and City B.
How many km is the distance between City B and City C?

After driving $90.3 km$ we used 10.5ℓ of gasoline.
How many km can we drive with 1ℓ of gasoline?

We bought a bag of clams as a souvenir for our friend. It cost 450 yen for $1.8 kg$. How much does $1 kg$ of clams cost?

R e v i e w · 2

① Please fill in the ⬭ with the appropriate numbers.

$4.385 = 1 \times \boxed{} + 0.1 \times \boxed{} + 0.01 \times \boxed{} + 0.001 \times \boxed{}$

② Please write the numbers that are 10 times, 100 times, $\frac{1}{10}$, and $\frac{1}{100}$ of the numbers below.

(1) 3.208　　　　　(2) 0.27　　　　　(3) 40.1

③ Please estimate first, then use a calculator to find the answers.

(1) 469 × 137　　(2) 91.1 × 203　　(3) 3.89 × 695

(4) 9861 ÷ 519　　(5) 703.5 ÷ 67　　(6) 960.4 ÷ 196

④ Please calculate the following.

(1) 3.2 × 4.7　　　(2) 7.3 × 0.6　　　(3) 2.89 × 5.6

(4) 43.5 × 7.2　　　(5) 8.7 × 7.23　　(6) 6.9 × 27.4

(7) 3.47 × 5.63　　(8) 0.72 × 3.86　　(9) 1.85 × 0.32

⑤ Please find the volumes of these shapes.

(1)

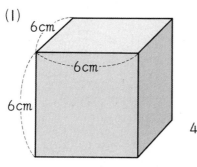

6cm
6cm
6cm

(2)

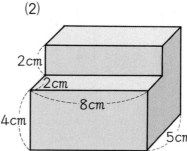

2cm
2cm
8cm
4cm
5cm

Congruent Shapes

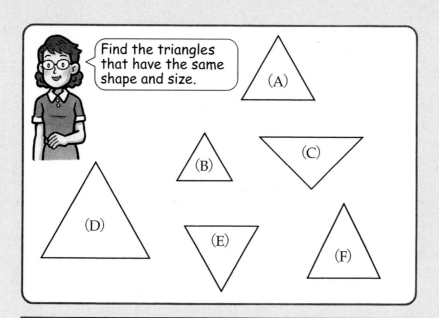

Find the triangles that have the same shape and size.

(A)

(B)

(C)

(D)

(E)

(F)

Let's investigate the characteristics of figures that have the same shape and size!

1 Congruent Shapes

1 **?** From the shapes below, which one has the same shape and size as figure A on the right?

(A)

(B)

(C)

(D)

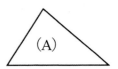

Copy the shape on tracing paper and . . .

1 Trace triangle A on a thin sheet of paper and lay it over figures B and D. Then, flip the paper and try again.

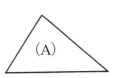 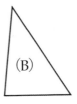

When two shapes can fit on top of each other perfectly, we say they are **congruent**.

Shapes that match after you flip them over are also congruent, aren't they?

1 Let's find two shapes that are congruent around you!

2 Let's find the congruent shapes!

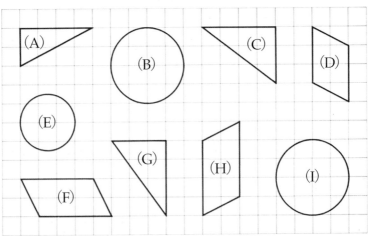

2 ❓ Two quadrilaterals, (A) and (B), are congruent. Let's investigate the vertices, sides, and angles that fit on top of each other!

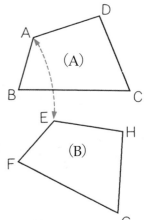

① With which vertex of quadrilateral (B) does each vertex of quadrilateral (A) match up?

On congruent figures, the vertices, sides, and angles which fit on top of each other are called **corresponding** vertices, corresponding sides, and corresponding angles.

② On quadrilaterals (A) and (B), please name the sides that correspond to sides BC and GH. Also name the corresponding angles of B and H.

❗ In congruent shapes, the lengths of the corresponding sides are equal. Also, the measures of the corresponding angles are the same.

① On the two quadrilaterals below, angles A and E, angles B and F, angles C and G, and angles D and H are equal. Are they congruent?

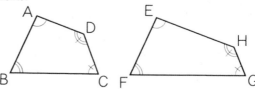

55

2 Of the quadrilaterals below, which will have congruent triangles when divided along a diagonal line?

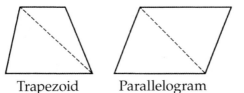 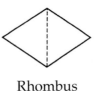

Trapezoid   Parallelogram   Rhombus

▶ **How to draw congruent triangles**

3 ❓ Let's think about how to draw a triangle A′B′C′ that is congruent to triangle ABC on the right!

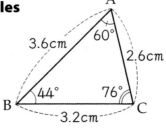

A
3.6cm 60°
2.6cm
44° 76°
B 3.2cm C

 Congruent triangles have corresponding sides of the same length, as well as corresponding angles of the same size.

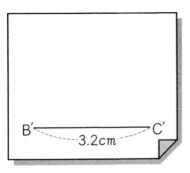

B′ 3.2cm C′

1 Draw a line segment B′C′ that has the same length as side BC above. How can we determine where to place vertex A′?

Besides side BC, there are 2 sides and 3 angles. Which ones should we use?

Yuji

2 Using the following three friends' methods, draw congruent triangles.

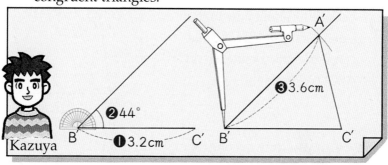

Kazuya

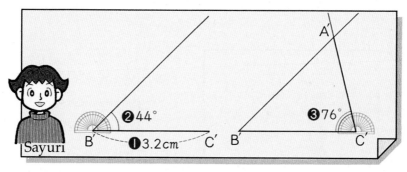

Sayuri

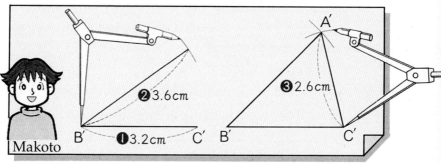

Makoto

> Without using all the sides and angles, we can draw congruent triangles, can't we?

1 Please draw an equilateral triangle that has sides that are 5cm.

▶ How to draw congruent quadrilaterals

4 Let's think about how to draw a quadrilateral A'B'C'D' that is congruent to quadrilateral ABCD on the right!

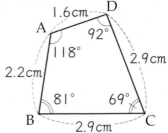

1 Can you draw a congruent guadrilateral by just using the length of the 4 sides?

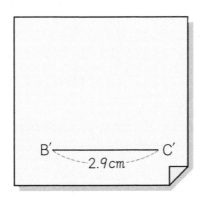

2 We drew a line B'C' that has the same length as side BC. How can we determine where to place vertices A' and D'?

3 Mami's and Minoru's thinking is shown below.
Please draw congruent quadrilaterals using their methods.

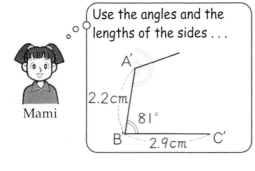

Use the angles and the lengths of the sides . . .

Mami

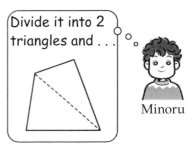

Divide it into 2 triangles and . . .

Minoru

2 Angles of Triangles and Quadrilaterals

▶ **The 3 angles of a triangle**

1 ❓ Let's investigate the 3 angles of a triangle!

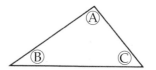

① Cut out the three congruent triangles on page 94 and place them as below.
Which angles would meet at point A?

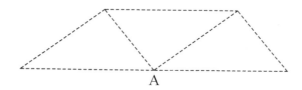

A

② What is the sum of the angles of those 3 angles?

③ Draw a triangle on paper and find the sum of the angles.

> Let's pick any shape and size triangle and investigate!

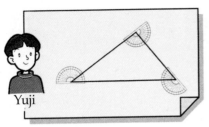
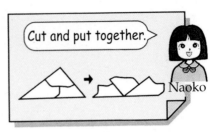

Cut and put together.

Yuji

Naoko

4　Using these two friends' methods, find the sum of the 3 angles of a triangle.

💡　The sum of the 3 angles of a triangle is 180°.

①　What is the size of angles Ⓐ and Ⓑ? Find them by calculation.

(1)

Ⓐ

50°　　　40°

(2)

Ⓑ

120°　　25°

▶ **The 4 angles of a quadrilateral**

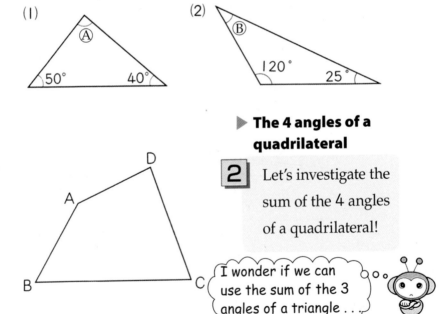

D

A

B　　　　　　C

2　Let's investigate the sum of the 4 angles of a quadrilateral!

I wonder if we can use the sum of the 3 angles of a triangle . . .

The sum of the 4 angles of a quadrilateral is 360°.

3 Let's find the number of sides, the number of vertices, and the sum of the angles of the following figures!

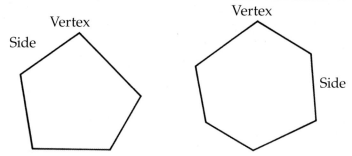

A shape surrounded by 5 straight lines is called a **pentagon** and a shape surrounded by 6 straight lines is called a **hexagon**.

Shapes that are surrounded by only straight lines such as triangles, quadrilaterals, pentagons, and hexagons are called **polygons**.

1 Find the number of sides and vertices of a pentagon. Then do the same for a hexagon.

2 Investigate the sum of the angles of a pentagon and a hexagon.

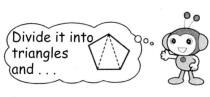

Divide it into triangles and . . .

3 Organize the results you found above in a table.

	Triangle	Quadrilateral	Pentagon	Hexagon
Number of Triangles	1			
Sum of Angles	180°			

① Which shapes are congruent to each other? Use a compass and a protractor to find out.

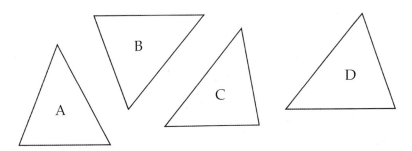

② Triangle ABC on the right is an isosceles triangle. What is the measure of angle A?

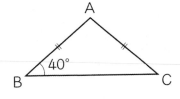

③ What is the sum of angles Ⓐ and Ⓑ?

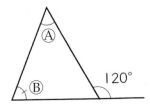

④ Find the angles Ⓐ, Ⓑ, and Ⓒ by calculation.

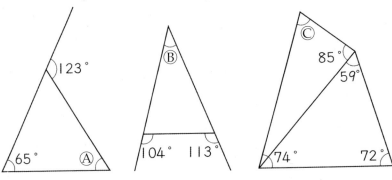

1. Fill in the ⬭ with the appropriate numbers and words.

(1) For congruent shapes, the lengths of [＿＿＿]
sides are [＿＿＿]. The size of the corresponding
[＿＿＿] are also [＿＿＿].

(2) The sum of the 3 angles of a triangle is [＿＿＿]°.

2. Please draw a triangle that is
congruent to the triangle on the
right by measuring the lengths of
the sides and the angles.

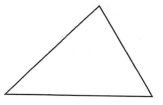

Challenge

There is a pair of figures with the same shape
below. Can you find it?

Please cut out the quadrilaterals on page 93 and lay them flat.

1. Using the congruent parallelograms, let's make different tiling patterns with no overlap or gaps!

There are many ways to tessellate . . .

2. Let's investigate whether we can make a tiling pattern with no overlap or gaps using the quadrilateral below!

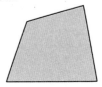

3 Let's create your own fun shape that can be used to make tiling patterns!

You can tessellate using a shape that is created from a parallelogram.

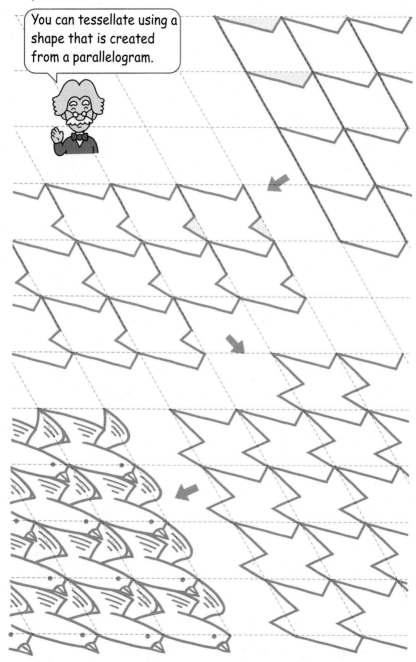

Making Shapes with Sticks

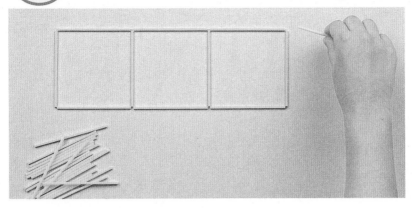

1 We are making squares using sticks that are the same length. If we build them as shown on the right, how many squares can we make with 31 sticks?

 When the number of squares increases by one, the number of sticks increases . . .

Number of squares	1	2	3	4	5	6	7
Number of sticks	4	7					

① We are making equilateral triangles using sticks that are the same length. If we build them as shown on the right, how many equilateral triangles can we make with 21 sticks?

How many sticks do we need to make 15 equilateral triangles?

① There is a container that has inside measures of 30cm length, 40cm width, and 20cm depth.
What is the capacity of the container in liters?

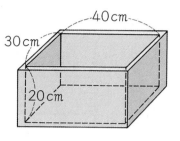

② Please do the following calculations.

(1) 7.4 × 5.3　　(2) 9.8 × 4.5　　(3) 6.5 × 0.8

(4) 1.82 × 5.4　　(5) 3.25 × 2.4　　(6) 8.35 × 2.02

③ Please divide completely.

(1) 108.1 ÷ 4.7　　(2) 32.64 ÷ 9.6　　(3) 32.4 ÷ 0.9

(4) 6.84 ÷ 5.7　　(5) 18.9 ÷ 0.45　　(6) 0.204 ÷ 8.5

(7) 9.62 ÷ 2.6　　(8) 4.176 ÷ 7.2　　(9) 36.85 ÷ 1.34

④ There are three different marathon courses, A, B, and C.
The distance of course B is 2.8km. The distance of course A is 1.2 times that of course B. The distance of course C is 0.8 times that of course B.

(1) Please find the distances of course A and course C.

(2) How many times is the distance of course A compared to the distance of course C?

6 Area of Quadrilaterals and Triangles

We have studied many different figures so far.

1 cm

1 cm

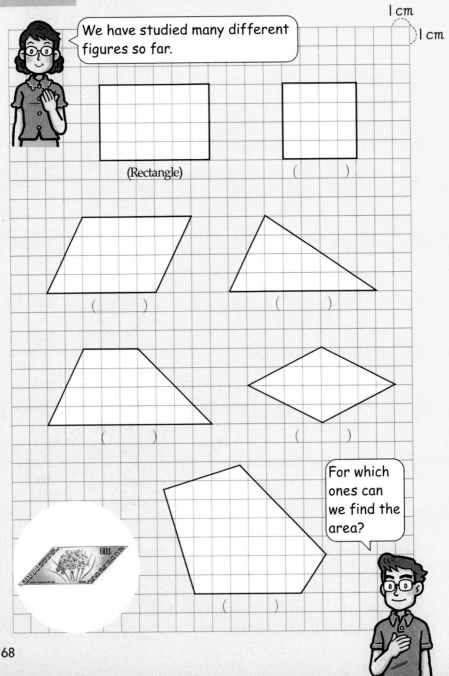

(Rectangle)

(   )

(   )

(   )

(   )

(   )

(   )

For which ones can we find the area?

x

68

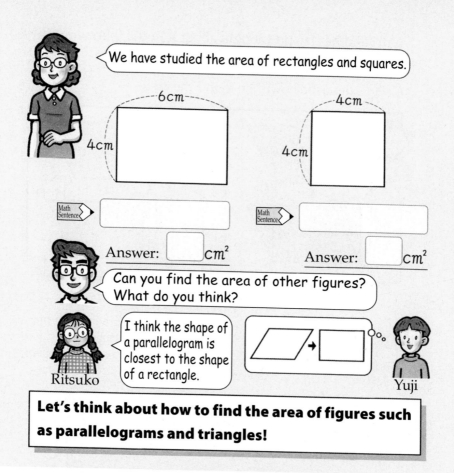

We have studied the area of rectangles and squares.

6cm
4cm

4cm
4cm

Math Sentence >

Answer: ☐ cm²

Math Sentence >

Answer: ☐ cm²

Can you find the area of other figures? What do you think?

Ritsuko: I think the shape of a parallelogram is closest to the shape of a rectangle.

Yuji

Let's think about how to find the area of figures such as parallelograms and triangles!

1 Area of Parallelograms

1 **?** Let's think about how to find the area of the following parallelogram!

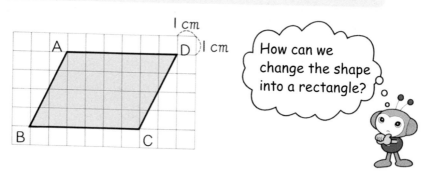

1 cm

A   D ☐ 1 cm

B   C

How can we change the shape into a rectangle?

Sayuri and her friend thought about it in the following ways:

1 Let's describe how they found the area!

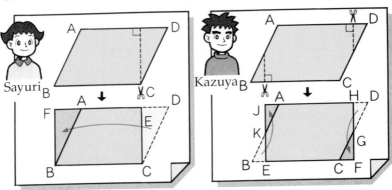

! The area of a parallelogram can be found by changing its shape into a rectangle.

> Even though the shape was changed, the area is still the same.

2 What is the length and width in cm of a rectangle with the same area as this parallelogram?

3 How many cm² is the area of this parallelogram?

▶ **The formula for finding the area of a parallelogram**

2 **?** Let's use Sayuri's method to think about a formula for finding the area of a parallelogram!

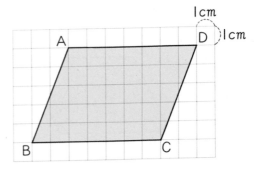

If we make side BC the **base**, a straight line that is perpendicular to the base, such as line AE, is called the **height**.

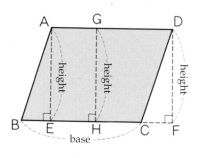

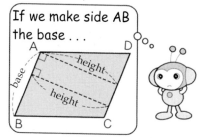

If we make side AB the base . . .

1　What part of the length of the parallelogram ABCD is equal to the length and the width of rectangle FBCE?

2　Let's find the area of parallelogram ABCD by calculation!

> The area of a parallelogram can be found using the following formula.
>
> **Area of Parallelogram=Base✕Height**

1　Let's find the area of the following parallelograms!

(1)

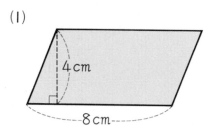

4 cm

8 cm

(2)

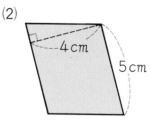

4 cm

5 cm

3 Let's think about how to find the area of the parallelogram on the right if we make side BC the base!

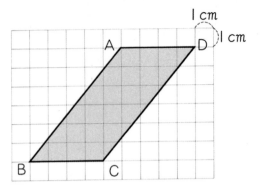

The height is located outside of the base, but I wonder if we can find the area in the same way.

1 Let's describe how they found the area!

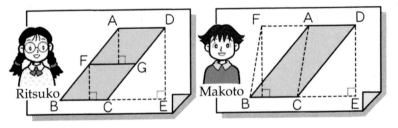

Ritsuko

Makoto

2 What is the area of parallelogram ABCD in cm²?

1 Let's find the area of the following parallelograms!

(1)

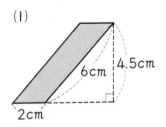

6cm 4.5cm

2cm

(2)

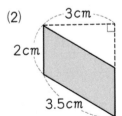

3cm

2cm

3.5cm

2 Area of Triangles

1 ❓ Let's think about how to find the area of the triangle below!

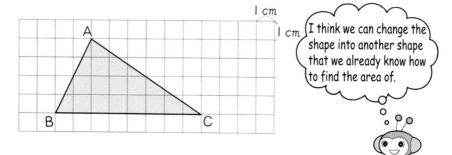

I think we can change the shape into another shape that we already know how to find the area of.

Yuji and his friends thought about it in the following ways.

⭐ 1 Let's describe their methods!

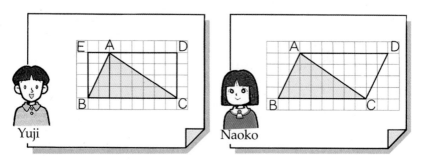

Yuji

Naoko

Minoru

What are the similarities and differences in these three methods?

⭐ 2 Let's calculate the area of the triangle above!

73

▶ The formula for the area of a triangle

2 ❓ Let's think about a formula for the area of a triangle by using Naoko's idea!

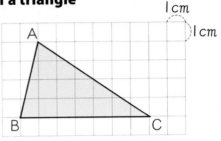

A straight line that is perpendiculor to the base is called the **height**.

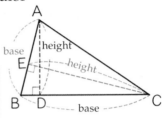

If we make side BC the base, the height is line AD.
If we make side AB the base, then the height is . . . .

1 What part of triangle ABC is the same as the length of the base and the height of parallelogram ABCD?

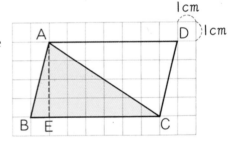

2 Let's calculate the area of triangle ABC!

❗ The area of a triangle can be found by using the following formula.

Area of Triangle＝Base×Height÷2

1 What are the areas of these triangles in cm^2?

(1)

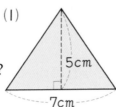
5cm
7cm

(2)

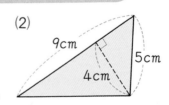
9cm
4cm
5cm

74

3 Let's think about how to find the area of the triangle on the right when you make side BC the base!

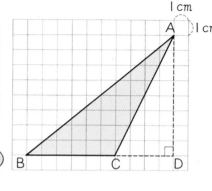

The height of the triangle is outside of the base. What can I do?

1 Please describe these two students' methods.

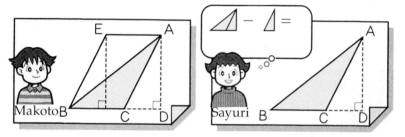

Makoto

Sayuri

2 How many cm^2 is the area of triangle ABC?

1 In the following diagram, two straight lines ℓ and m are parallel lines. The area of triangle ABC is always the same no matter where vertex A is located as long as it is on line ℓ. Please describe the reason why the area of these triangles is always the same.

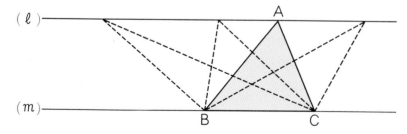

① Please measure the necessary parts of the following figures and find their areas.

(1)

(2)

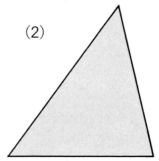

② The parallel lines are equally spaced and the distance between the lines is 1 cm. Please compare the areas of these two parallelograms, Ⓐ and Ⓑ.

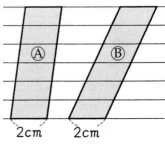

2cm   2cm

③ This diagram for triangle ABC contains 2 sets of base and height. Please describe each set of base and height.
Then please find the area of the triangle.

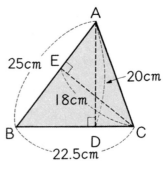

④ Please find the area of the triangle on the right.

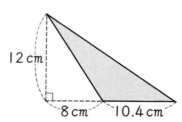

12 cm

8 cm   10.4 cm

3 Area of Various Quadrilaterals

1 ❷ Let's think about the area of the following trapezoid!

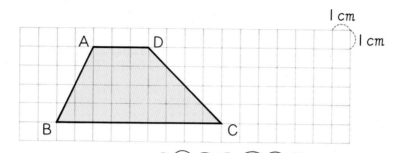

1 cm
1 cm

> We can change the shape into other shapes that we already know how to find the areas of.

Mami and her friends thought about it in the following ways.

1 Let's describe these three friends' ideas!

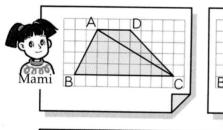

Mami

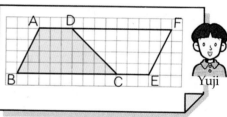

Yuji

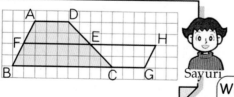

Sayuri

> What part of their ideas are similar or different?

2 Let's find the area of the trapezoid above by calculation!

▶ The formula for the area of a trapezoid

2 🔢 Let's think about a formula for the area of a trapezoid by using Yuji's idea!

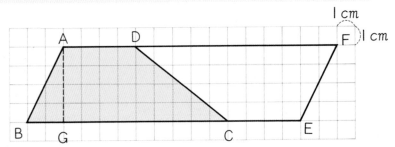

In trapezoid ABCD on the right, sides AD and BC are parallel. AD is called the **top base** and the BC is called the **bottom base**. Straight lines that are perpendicular to the top and bottom bases, such as line AG, are called the height.

1 The base BE of parallelogram ABEF is equal to the sum of which sides of trapezoid ABCD?

2 Let's find the area of trapezoid ABCD above by calculation!

> 💡 The area of a trapezoid can be found by using the following formula.
>
> **Area of Trapezoid = (Top Base + Bottom Base) × Height ÷ 2**

1 How many cm² are the areas of these trapezoids on the right?

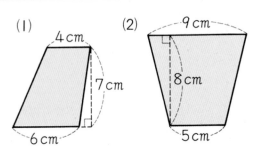

Methods for Finding the Area and Their Formula.

Can you develop formulas using Mami's and Sayuri's ideas?

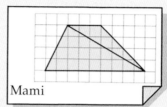

Mami

Let's develop the formula for the area of a trapezoid from Mami's and Sayuri's ideas!

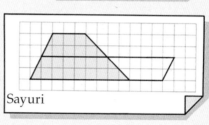

Sayuri

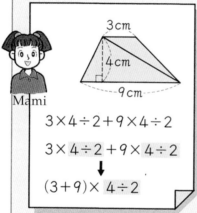

Mami

3cm
4cm
9cm

$3 \times 4 \div 2 + 9 \times 4 \div 2$

$3 \times 4 \div 2 + 9 \times 4 \div 2$

↓

$(3 + 9) \times 4 \div 2$

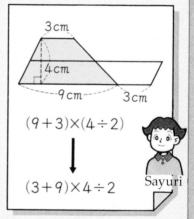

3cm
4cm
9cm
3cm

$(9 + 3) \times (4 \div 2)$

↓

$(3 + 9) \times 4 \div 2$

Sayuri

(Top Base + Bottom Base) × Height ÷ 2

Can we construct the formula for the area of a triangle with Yuji's and Minoru's ideas on page 73?

Practice 2

① Please compare the areas of parallelogram ABEF and trapezoid ABCD.

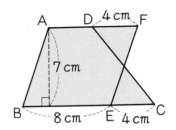

② Please find the area of the shaded part.

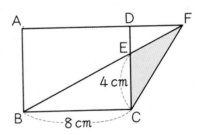

③ The area of rectangle ABCD is $48\ cm^2$. If line EC is $4cm$, what is the area of triangle ECF in cm^2?

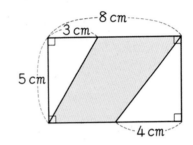

④ Please find the area of the shaded part in various ways.

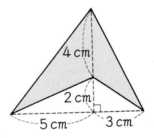

Check

1 Please find the area of the parallelogram, triangle, and trapezoid below.

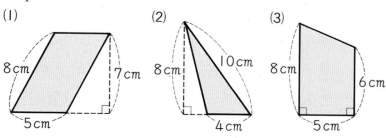

(1)

8 cm

7 cm

5 cm

(2)

8 cm

10 cm

4 cm

(3)

8 cm

6 cm

5 cm

Challenge

Moving Area

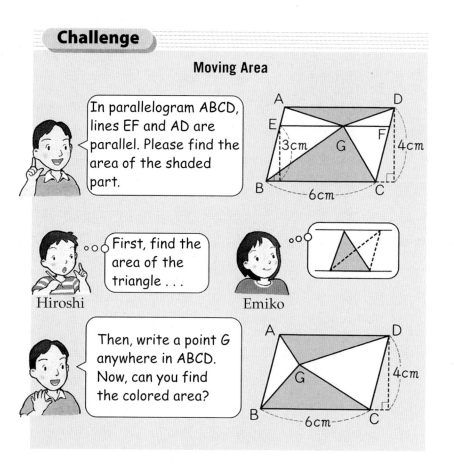

In parallelogram ABCD, lines EF and AD are parallel. Please find the area of the shaded part.

A   D

E

3cm   G   F   4cm

B   ——6cm——   C

First, find the area of the triangle . . .

Hiroshi

Emiko

Then, write a point G anywhere in ABCD. Now, can you find the colored area?

A   D

G   4cm

B   ——6cm——   C

4 Ideas for Finding the Area

▶ **How to find the area of polygons**

1 Let's think about ideas for finding the area of a pentagon!

I wonder if we can use the formulas we have learned so far.

1 Let's make triangles using diagonal lines and find the area of a pentagon!

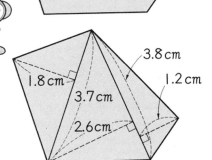

We can find the area of any polygon if we use this method!

① Let's find the area of the shaded part!

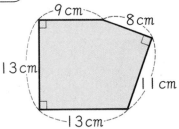

② Let's think about how to find the area of the rhombus! What is the area?

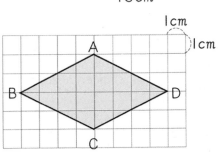

▶ Estimating area

2 There is a leaf shaped like the figure on the right. Let's think about how to estimate the area of this leaf!

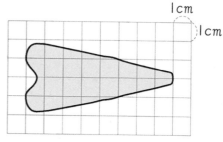

1 cm

1 cm

1 Please estimate the area of the leaf using Minoru's and Naoko's methods.

Minoru

Think about a shape that is close to the shape of the leaf.

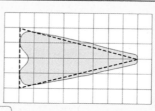

The shape looks like a [　　　　].

[　　] × [　　] ÷ 2 = [　　]　Answer: About [　　] cm²

Naoko

I counted squares of the graph paper.

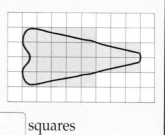

❶ The number of squares which are completely inside of the leaf ⋯⋯ [　　] squares

❷ The number of squares which are not completely inside ⋯⋯ [　　] squares

Think about squares that are not completely inside as half squares.

[　　] + [　　] ÷ 2 = [　　]　Answer: About [　　] cm²

83

R e v i e w · 4

① Please do the following calculations. For the division calculations divide completely.

(1) 6.7×5.8 (2) 0.62×3.5 (3) 2.8×0.76

(4) 0.55×8.9 (5) 13.7×0.48 (6) 7.16×2.14

(7) $25.2 \div 0.6$ (8) $663 \div 8.5$ (9) $655.5 \div 1.9$

(10) $16.2 \div 0.25$ (11) $3.22 \div 4.6$ (12) $59.52 \div 1.28$

② Please find the volume of the following.

   (1) A cube with $9cm$ edges

   (2) A rectangular prism with $8cm$ length, $5cm$ width, and $7cm$ height

   (3) A rectangular prism with $3.5m$ length, $2.8m$ width, and $4m$ height

③ Please draw a congruent triangle to triangle ABC on the right.

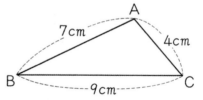

④ Please find the measure of angles Ⓐ and Ⓑ by calculation.

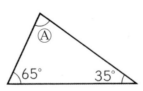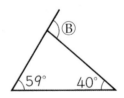

⑤ The distance from Town A to Town B is $58.2km$. The distance from Town A to Town C is $203.7km$. How many times is the distance from Town A to Town C as the distance from Town A to Town B?

84

7 Variables and Mathematical Equations

There are many parallelograms which have a height of 4cm. Find math sentences to find the area of these shapes.

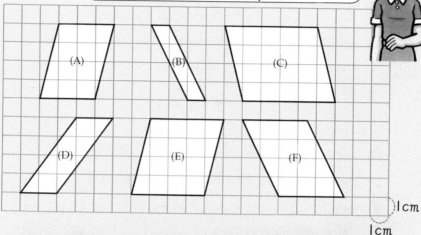

1cm
1cm

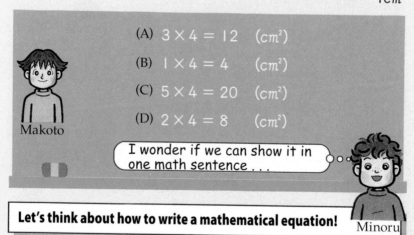

(A) $3 \times 4 = 12$ (cm²)

(B) $1 \times 4 = 4$ (cm²)

(C) $5 \times 4 = 20$ (cm²)

(D) $2 \times 4 = 8$ (cm²)

Makoto

I wonder if we can show it in one math sentence . . .

Let's think about how to write a mathematical equation! Minoru

▶ Mathematical equations using variables

1 Let's discuss how to write a mathematical equation that shows the area of many different kinds of parallelograms that have heights of 4cm!

1 Please write a math sentence for the area using the length of the base as ▢cm and the area as ◯cm².

$$\square \times 4 = \bigcirc$$

When you write a mathematical equation, you may use x and y instead of symbols like ▢ and ◯, and write it in the following way.

$$\square \times 4 = \bigcirc \quad \rightarrow \quad x \times 4 = y$$

2 Using the mathematical equation $x \times 4 = y$, please find y when x is 10, 15, 20, and 4.5.

3 In the mathematical equation $x \times 4 = y$, for what value of x do you have $x \times 4 = 52$?

> The area of a parallelogram with a height of 4 cm can be written in one mathematical equation, $x \times 4 = y$.

1 Besides using the mathematical equation $x \times 4 = y$ to find the area of a parallelogram with a height of 4cm, what other relationships can you show with this equation?

> The same volume of juice . . .

Yuji

2 $x\,d\ell$ of juice is shared equally by 4 people. If $y\,d\ell$ is the amount each person gets, find a mathematical equation that shows the relationship between x and y.

> Let's use x and y for many different problem solving situations in the future!

▶ Problems involving finding the value of x

2 The area of the 5th graders' flower garden is 4.4m². The area is 0.8 times the area of the 6th graders' flower garden. Let's find the area of the 6th graders' flower garden!

1 Make the area of the 6th graders' flower garden $x\,m^2$ and write a mathematical equation with multiplication.

2 Please find the value of x.

$$x \times 0.8 = 4.4$$

$$x = 4.4 \div 0.8$$

$$x = \boxed{} \qquad \text{Answer:} \underline{\boxed{}\,m^2}$$

3 Put the answer above into the mathematical equation $x \times 0.8 = 4.4$ and check the answer.

① Please find the values of x in the following mathematical equations.

(1) $76 + x = 96$ (2) $25 \times x = 200$ (3) $x \div 3 = 7$

② There is a triangle with a height of 4cm and an area of 16cm².

Please set the length of the base as $x\,cm$, and construct a mathematical equation. Then find the length of the base.

87

Let's Make a Plan!

1 Emiko and her friends are planning a trip for the next holiday.

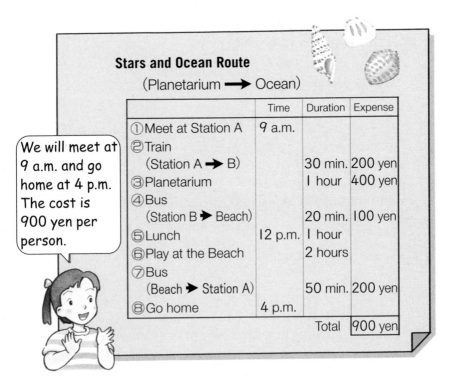

Stars and Ocean Route
(Planetarium ➡ Ocean)

	Time	Duration	Expense
① Meet at Station A	9 a.m.		
② Train (Station A ➡ B)		30 min.	200 yen
③ Planetarium		1 hour	400 yen
④ Bus (Station B ➡ Beach)		20 min.	100 yen
⑤ Lunch	12 p.m.	1 hour	
⑥ Play at the Beach		2 hours	
⑦ Bus (Beach ➡ Station A)		50 min.	200 yen
⑧ Go home	4 p.m.		
		Total	900 yen

We will meet at 9 a.m. and go home at 4 p.m. The cost is 900 yen per person.

Plan different routes for the trip and calculate the time and cost.

Calculation Practice

① (1) 6.59 × 9.3　　(2) 0.82 × 0.74　　(3) 16 × 5.02

(4) 7.5 × 5.44　　(5) 13.4 × 4.2　　(6) 5.36 × 37.5

(7) 1.65 × 91　　(8) 3.88 × 0.27　　(9) 2.9 × 0.28

(10) 0.056 × 7.5　　(11) 24 × 41.7　　(12) 0.18 × 0.37

(13) 3.15 × 0.32　　(14) 8.6 × 4.07　　(15) 29.2 × 89

(16) 8.5 × 80.3　　(17) 48 × 0.95　　(18) 8.14 × 27.3

(19) 0.065 × 420　　(20) 0.75 × 0.096　　(21) 58 × 4.85

(22) 4.7 × 0.64　　(23) 850 × 2.36　　(24) 0.036 × 1.5

② (1) 9.62 ÷ 3.7　　(2) 2.709 ÷ 4.3　　(3) 24 ÷ 3.75

(4) 6.9 ÷ 0.75　　(5) 46.62 ÷ 0.63　　(6) 9.006 ÷ 2.37

(7) 72.8 ÷ 2.8　　(8) 27 ÷ 0.25　　(9) 4.028 ÷ 5.3

(10) 2.4 ÷ 0.96　　(11) 6.96 ÷ 0.87　　(12) 8.652 ÷ 4.2

(13) 21.28 ÷ 0.07　　(14) 3 ÷ 62.5　　(15) 73.1 ÷ 0.86

(16) 7.47 ÷ 8.3　　(17) 5.1 ÷ 0.24　　(18) 44.18 ÷ 9.4

①	0.812	1.008	0.6068	1.0476	27.3	80.32	40.8
	0.42	150.15	56.28	61.287	201	222.222	0.0666
	2006		0.072	682.55		3.008	45.6
	0.054		2598.8	35.002		1000.8	281.3
②	85	9.2	3.8	0.63	304	4.7	74	0.76
	2.6	0.9	26	6.4	108	2.5	8	0.048
	2.06	21.25						

Please color the answers.

90

③ (1) $1.6 + 0.62 \times 3.5$　　　(2) $8.9 - 10.35 \div 2.3$

(3) $(5.8 + 1.36) \times 2.14$　　(4) $(5.57 - 1.28) \div 15.6$

(5) $10.56 \div (1.82 + 3.46)$　(6) $6.41 \times (1.08 - 0.95)$

(7) $(11.01 - 2.46) \times 0.98$　(8) $(1.908 + 0.885) \div 0.57$

(9) $52.7 \div (40.4 - 7.6 \times 4.5)$

(10) $301.4 - 0.56 \times 22.5 + 11.43$

④ Please round off the quotients to the nearest $\frac{1}{10}$.

(1) $9.45 \div 5.7$　　　(2) $6.71 \div 0.83$　　　(3) $2.6 \div 3.5$

(4) $46 \div 3.72$　　　(5) $2.08 \div 4.2$　　　(6) $6.72 \div 0.76$

(7) $1.17 \div 2.8$　　　(8) $7.28 \div 0.37$　　　(9) $27 \div 4.19$

⑤ Please find the quotients to one decimal place and show the remainders.

(1) $5.2 \div 0.84$　　　(2) $4.14 \div 2.2$　　　(3) $29.57 \div 0.73$

(4) $2.33 \div 2.7$　　　(5) $78 \div 8.4$　　　(6) $3.16 \div 6.38$

(7) $48.7 \div 3.6$　　　(8) $9.8 \div 0.43$　　　(9) $32 \div 4.75$

③	300.23	2	3.77	8.379	0.275	8.5			
	4.4	15.3224		0.8333	4.9				
④	0.7	19.7	0.5	8.8	6.4	12.4	1.7	8.1	0.4
	0.8	R 0.17		1.8	R 0.18		22.7	R 0.039	
⑤	40.5	R 0.005		6.7	R 0.175		9.2	R 0.72	
	0.4	R 0.608		6.1	R 0.076		13.5	R 0.1	

Editorial supervisors

Heisuke Hironaka Professor of Mathematics Kyoto University(Emeritus) Harvard University(Emeritus)

Yoshishige Sugiyama Professor of Mathematics Education Tokyo Gakugei University(Emeritus)

Cover design / Ryoichi Minagawa, Shizuko Minagawa, (Photographs)Yoshinori Watabe

Interior design / Katsuya Hirose, Tetsuhiro Urakawa

Illustrations and Photos / Akagawa Design, Satsuki Inukai, Koji Okutani,
Nobuyoshi Kurosawa, Minoru Zama, Akiko Shibata, Kosei Tamura, Akio Tsuzuki,
Arinobu Fukushima, Jun Yamashina, CTS Photonica, JTB Photo,Sekai Bunka Photo,
All M.C.Escher work © Cordon Art B.V.-Baarn-the Netherlands, Huis Ten Bosch

Translators / **Makoto Yoshida** Global Education Resources (Senior Project Director)

Akihiko Takahashi DePaul University (Project Director)

Tad Watanabe The Pennsylvania State University (Project Director)

William C. Jackson, Ⅲ Paterson Public School No.2

Mary N. Leer School District of Lancaster

Jennifer L. Shouffler Teaneck Public Schools

Mathematics 5A for Elementary School

the date of issue 2/20/2006

Editors **Heisuke Hironaka, Yoshishige Sugiyama** and 36 professors and teachers

Publisher **Tokyo Shoseki Co., Ltd.** 2-17-1 HORIFUNE, KITA-KU, TOKYO, JAPAN

Printer **Tokyo Shoseki Printing Co., Ltd.** 1-23-31 HORIFUNE, KITA-KU, TOKYO, JAPAN

Phone International Department +81(3)5390-7513

代表

広中平祐 京都大学名誉教授・ハーバード大学名誉教授   杉山吉茂 東京学芸大学名誉教授

表紙 皆川良一／皆川静子／(撮影)渡部佳則   本文デザイン 広瀬克也・浦川哲広(㈱コッフェル)

さし絵・図版・写真 赤川デザイン／いぬかい さつき／奥谷耕次／黒沢信義／座間実／
　　　柴田亜樹子／田村公生／都築昭夫／福島有伸／山科潤／
　　　CTSフォトニカ／JTBフォト／世界文化フォト／
　　　All M.C.Escher work © Cordon Art B.V.-Baarn-the Netherlands, Huis Ten Bosch

翻訳 吉田誠 Global Education Resources(Senior Project Director)／高橋昭彦 ディポール大学助教授／
　　　Tad Watanabe ペンシルベニア州立大学教授／William C. Jackson, Ⅲ Paterson Public School No.2／
　　　Mary N. Leer School District of Lancaster／Jennifer L. Shouffler Teaneck Public Schools

新訂 新しい算数　5上

平成18年2月20日発行

著作者 広中平祐・杉山吉茂 ほか36名

発行者 東京書籍株式会社   代表者 河内義勝   東京都北区堀船2丁目17番1号

印刷者 東京書籍印刷株式会社   代表者 星　永揚   東京都北区堀船2丁目23番31号

発行所 東京書籍株式会社   東京都北区堀船2丁目17番1号　〒114-8524

電話 本社 広報 03-5390-7212 編集 03-5390-7386 供給・販売 03-5390-7247
　　 支社・出張所 札幌 011-562-5721 仙台 022-297-2666 東京 03-5390-7467 金沢 076-222-7581 名古屋 052-211-2323
　　　　　　　　　大阪 06-6397-1350 広島 082-568-2577 福岡 092-771-1536 那覇 098-834-8084